# GREAT BATTLES AND SIEGES

PHILIP SAUVAIN

ILLUSTRATIONS BY
**TONY GIBBONS**

New York

Maxwell Macmillan Canada
Toronto

Maxwell Macmillan International
New York • Oxford • Singapore • Sydney

# GREAT BATTLES

First American publication 1993 by New Discovery Books, Macmillan Publishing Company, 866 Third Avenue, New York, NY 10022
Maxwell Macmillan Canada Inc., 1200 Eglinton Avenue East, Suite 200, Don Mills, Ontario M3C 3N1

Macmillan Publishing Company is part of the Maxwell Communication Group of Companies.

First published in 1993 in Great Britain by
Zoë Books Limited
15 Worthy Lane
Winchester
Hampshire SO23 7AB
England

## A ZOË BOOK

Devised and produced by
Zoë Books Limited
15 Worthy Lane
Winchester
Hampshire SO23 7AB
England

Printed in Italy
Design: Julian Holland Publishing Ltd
Picture research: Victoria Sturgess
Illustrations: Tony Gibbons
Production: Grahame Griffiths

10 9 8 7 6 5 4 3 2 1

Library of Congress Cataloging-in-Publication Data
Sauvain, Philip Arthur.
  Midway/by Philip Sauvain.
  p.   cm. — (Great battles and sieges)
Includes bibliographical references and index.
  Summary: Describes the events leading up to the Battle of Midway, the battle itself, and the aftermath.
  ISBN 0-02-781090-9
  1. Midway, Battle of, 1942—Juvenile literature. [1. Midway, Battle of, 1942. 2. World War, 1939-1945—Campaigns.] I. Title. II. Series.
  D774.M5S26   1993
  940.54'26—dc20                              92-29566

### Photographic acknowledgments

The publishers wish to acknowledge, with thanks, the following photographic sources:
Camera Press 23b; National Archives, Washington D.C. 20, 21, 23t; Peter Newark's Military Pictures 7, 9, 11, 12, 14, 18, 19t, 22, 24, 25, 26, 27b; Quadrant/Flight 13; Topham Picture Source 10, 16, 19b, 27t, 28, 29; Copyright Twentieth Century Fox, courtesy of the Kobal Collection 6

# MIDWAY

# Contents

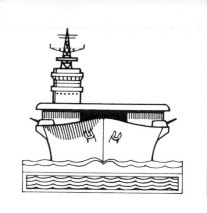

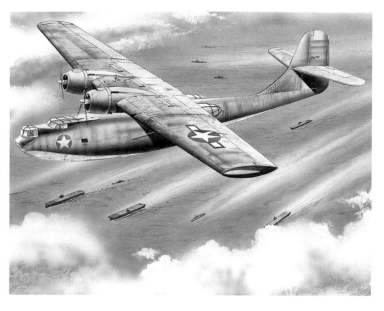

# Five Minutes That Changed History

Midmorning, June 4, 1942. For some time the 37 Dauntless **dive-bombers,** led by Lieutenant Commander Wade McClusky, had been searching the blue seas of the Pacific Ocean. Flying high in the sky at about 19,000 feet (6,000 meters), they were looking for the Japanese **aircraft carriers** that had launched air attacks on **Midway,** two tiny islands that the U.S. Navy used as a base. Then McClusky spotted a Japanese **destroyer** steaming ahead at full speed. As an experienced pilot, he knew that this must be one of the warships defending the Japanese carriers against attack from the sea. He decided to follow it.

## Following the Trail

McClusky was right. Far below him, he caught sight of his prey. These were the Japanese aircraft carriers *Akagi, Kaga, Soryu,* and *Hiryu.* McClusky and his men knew there was no time to lose. Any minute now they could expect to see Japan's much-feared Zero **fighter** planes streaming toward them. The Zeros (sometimes called Zekes) were the best fighter planes in the Pacific at that time. They patroled the skies above the Japanese aircraft carriers, and they were fast and deadly in combat.

What McClusky did not know, however, was that the Zeros had been fighting off earlier attacks made by low-flying squadrons of American Devastator **torpedo bombers.** Some of the Zeros were reloading fuel and ammunition on board the carriers. Others were still flying too close to sea level to be of any use when the dive-bombers attacked. To be effective, they had to be higher in the sky than their opponents.

## The American Attack

At 10:24 A.M. the American attack began. It changed the course of history. It turned the war between the United States and Japan in favor of the Americans. McClusky's Dauntless bombers screamed down on the four Japanese aircraft carriers far below. The Japanese antiaircraft gunners were unable to stop them. On board the carriers there was shock and confusion. The **flight decks** of these huge **flattops,** as they were called, provided the American pilots with unmissable targets. What was worse, from the Japanese point of view, the carriers were crowded with aircraft carrying fuel and explosives. The ships were like powder kegs. One spark and they would explode.

For about five minutes, bombs rained down on the *Akagi, Kaga,* and *Soryu.* All three carriers were damaged beyond repair and sank within 24 hours. In those few minutes, McClusky's men had destroyed one third of the entire Japanese carrier fleet.

▶ *10:25 A.M. Thursday, June 4, 1942. American Dauntless dive-bombers begin their attack on the Japanese carrier **fleet**.*

# "Tora! Tora! Tora!"

The destruction of the Japanese aircraft carriers at Midway came almost exactly six months after the disaster at **Pearl Harbor** on December 7, 1941. This was the day when the people of the United States had been plunged into war, first against Japan and then, within days, against Hitler's Germany.

At the start of 1941 the United States and the Soviet Union were not part of World War II, which was raging in Europe and North Africa. The Americans, however, were very concerned about another war, in the Far East. Japan and China had been fighting each other since 1937, and Japan was an ally of Hitler. The United States had helped China in fighting this war. As a result, American relations with Japan were getting steadily worse.

In June 1941, Hitler launched a savage and unexpected attack on the Soviet Union. He took Russia's leader, Joseph Stalin, completely by surprise. The attack was a warning to the Americans as well. Although people were talking about going to war with Japan, the American troops defending Pearl Harbor were still caught by surprise.

▼ *This still photograph was taken when the movie* Tora! Tora! Tora! *was being filmed. The movie tells the story of the Japanese attack on Pearl Harbor.*

# MIDWAY

◄ *Eight American battleships were sunk or badly damaged during the raid on Pearl Harbor. Here you can see some of the destruction the raid caused. The battleships* Tennessee *and* West Virginia *are on fire.*

## The Attack on Pearl Harbor

Pearl Harbor was a large American naval base in the **Hawaiian Islands** in the middle of the Pacific Ocean. Although peace talks were being held between the United States and Japan in Washington, the **Japanese High Command** had secretly sent a fleet of six aircraft carriers and supporting warships toward Hawaii. They were under the command of **Admiral** Chuichi Nagumo. When his ships were still several hundred miles from Pearl Harbor, he launched his attack. Japanese warplanes swooped low over Hawaii early on Sunday morning, December 7, 1941. The American defenses were not prepared for a lightning attack like this. At first the sailors, marines, soldiers, and their families at the base did not understand what was happening. No one had declared war. They were supposed to be at peace.

## The United States Enters the War

President Franklin Delano Roosevelt called it "a date which will live in infamy." Four American **battleships** were sunk; and another four were badly damaged. Nearly 200 warplanes were destroyed on the ground and more than 2,300 American civilians and servicemen and -women were killed. When the commander of the Japanese attack force could see that the raid had been successful, he sent a **radio signal** back to Admiral Nagumo: *"Tora! Tora! Tora!"* ("Tiger! Tiger! Tiger!")

Japan was now at war with the United States. Britain and the countries of the **Commonwealth** also declared war on Japan, while Germany and Italy declared war on the United States. Pearl Harbor had been a terrible disaster for the United States. There was sorrow at the deaths of so many innocent people, and fury and anger because the Japanese had not declared war before the attack.

# At War in Southeast Asia

The attack on Pearl Harbor was not a complete success. The Japanese commander in chief, Admiral Isoroku Yamamoto, had hoped to sink all the American aircraft carriers as well as the battleships. Had this been achieved, the Japanese navy would have been masters of the Pacific Ocean. They could then have threatened Hawaii and the West Coast of the United States.

The three U.S. aircraft carriers that were based at Pearl Harbor — the *Lexington, Saratoga,* and *Enterprise* — were all at sea at the time of the attack. They lived to fight another day. They were joined by two new carriers, the *Yorktown* and the *Hornet.* These five ships made it possible for the United States to fight back. The successful attack at Midway, less than six months later, was due in large part to the skill and leadership of the new U.S. commander in chief in the Pacific, Admiral Chester Nimitz.

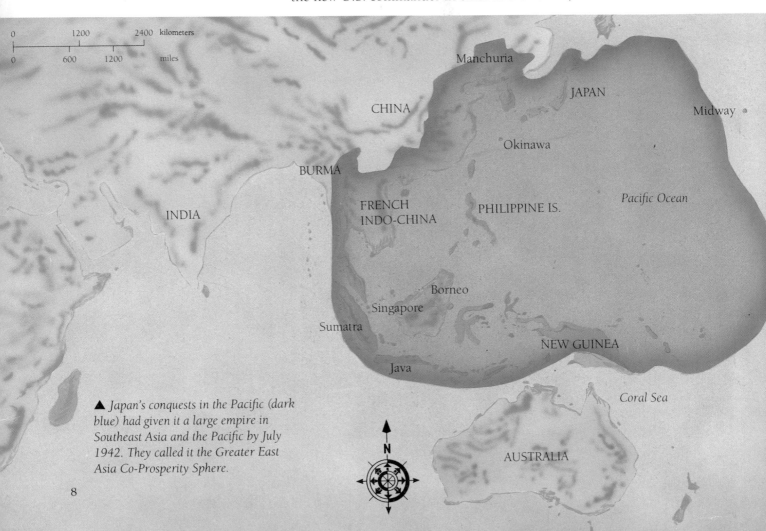

▲ *Japan's conquests in the Pacific (dark blue) had given it a large empire in Southeast Asia and the Pacific by July 1942. They called it the Greater East Asia Co-Prosperity Sphere.*

# MIDWAY

After Pearl Harbor, the Japanese went on to seize Hong Kong, Malaysia, Singapore, Burma, the Philippines, many Pacific islands, and the Dutch East Indies. In less than six months, the Japanese flag flew over a quarter of the world's surface. People living in Hawaii, Australia, and India began to fear that the Japanese might seize their lands as well.

## The Battle of the Coral Sea

This brilliant series of Japanese victories came to a halt in May 1942 at the Battle of the Coral Sea, off the coast of Australia. This sea battle was fought between May 4 and 8, 1942. It was a most unusual battle. It was the first in naval history in which the enemy ships were out of sight of each other throughout the fighting. The battle itself was fought in the air by warplanes launched from aircraft carriers.

In the end, there was no outright winner, although the Allies probably came off best. Each side gained some advantages and suffered some losses. One American aircraft carrier, the *Lexington,* was sunk, and another, the *Yorktown,* was badly damaged. Japan, too, lost an aircraft carrier, the *Shoho,* and two other carriers, the *Shokaku* and *Zuikaku,* were badly damaged in the action. For the moment, the Japanese had to abandon any idea of invading Australia and southern New Guinea.

▲ *Admiral Nimitz inspects the American air and naval base on Midway.*

◄ *The most important victim of the Battle of the Coral Sea was the U.S. aircraft carrier* Lexington. *The ship was so badly damaged that the crew had to abandon ship. More than 2,500 men were saved but 216 died.*

# The First Air Raid on Tokyo

On April 18, 1942, an unfamiliar sound was heard in the streets of Tokyo, the capital of Japan. American **B-25** bombers flying low over the city were dropping bombs. It was Japan's first air raid. The Japanese people were shocked. Suddenly it brought home to them that despite their victories, they could still be attacked from the air. Many people regarded the raid as a great insult to the emperor. To the Japanese people at that time, Emperor Hirohito was a god. Japanese military leaders apologized to the emperor for the air raid!

▲ *Colonel (later General) James Doolittle of the U.S. Air Force led the daring raid on Tokyo on April 18, 1942. A report that one of his twin-engined bombers had been seen approaching Japan was dismissed by the Japanese High Command. They knew that there were no aircraft with two engines on American aircraft carriers.*

*Although the Doolittle bombing raid on Tokyo did very little damage, it gave the American people and their allies a very welcome boost.*

# MIDWAY

◀ *U.S. marines on Midway during the war. Midway is a coral reef with two islands, occupying a total land area of little more than two square miles (five square kilometers).*

## A Surprise Attack

How had the Americans done it? The B-25 bombers could fly only a certain distance before refueling, and there were no American air bases close enough for this. In fact, the bombers took off from the aircraft carrier *Hornet*, when it was about 620 miles (1,000 kilometers) off the coast of Japan. Colonel (later General) James Doolittle of the U.S. Air Force led his planes low over the sea and across Japan. They had planned to land at friendly bases in China, but some of the planes ran out of fuel and had to crash-land.

This first air raid on Tokyo did little damage, but it warned the Japanese that the Americans, only four months after Pearl Harbor, were capable of launching surprise attacks of their own. The attack also raised the spirits of the Americans and their allies, as President Roosevelt had hoped. The Japanese High Command knew that the U.S. bombers must have taken off from an aircraft carrier. This was upsetting, because it showed that the U.S. Navy was still a threat to Japanese plans to control the Pacific. Until the U.S. ships were sunk, Japan would not feel safe from attack. This is why Yamamoto and his naval staff planned an attack on Midway and the **Aleutians**, in the middle of the Pacific Ocean. They hoped to use the attack to trap the U.S. Navy and to destroy American sea power. Midway could then be used as a Japanese base from which to invade Hawaii itself.

Midway is just a tiny dot in the middle of the Pacific Ocean. Although part of the Hawaiian Islands, it is some 1,116 miles (1,800 kilometers) to the northwest of Pearl Harbor. At that time it was used by the United States as an ammunition dump, fuel depot, and air and naval base. There were no trees there to offer shelter—just a runway, some aircraft **hangars**, and a number of military buildings. There were also 150 aircraft at Midway, but many of these were no match for the Japanese warplanes.

# Admiral Yamamoto's Plans

"I am looking forward to dictating peace to the United States in the White House at Washington"
— *ADMIRAL YAMAMOTO*

What do YOU say, AMERICA?

▲ *This American propaganda poster was printed in 1942. Admiral Isoroku Yamamoto was one of Japan's ablest commanders. One writer said that killing him in 1943 was the same as winning a great battle.*

Admiral Yamamoto and his advisers thought up a complicated plan using almost all the warships in the Japanese navy. Instead of launching an all-out attack, they chose a plan that involved a number of separate groups of ships.

First, there was an invasion fleet commanded by Admiral Nobukato Kondo. This was a special group, called a **task force**. It consisted of transport ships carrying 5,000 soldiers. Battleships, cruisers, and destroyers protected the transport ships. The army would land on Midway and turn it into a Japanese air and naval base. It could do this, however, only when the U.S. aircraft on Midway were put out of action. This job was given to the warplanes carried by a fleet of four aircraft carriers. The carrier fleet was commanded by Admiral Nagumo, the successful commander at Pearl Harbor. Nagumo's first job was to destroy the base at Midway and then go on to destroy the U.S. Navy.

## Yamamoto's Trap

Other commanders were in charge of groups of merchant ships bringing fuel and supplies, **minesweepers,** and other supporting ships. Yamamoto himself took command of the operation from the *Yamato*, the world's biggest battleship. Yamamoto thought that their great **firepower** could easily destroy any American warships that might be sent to recapture Midway. He believed that the Americans would have to send their navy to rescue the islands, in order to protect Hawaii. When they fell into this

▶ *This map shows how Yamamoto planned to attack Midway. He hoped to lure the U.S. aircraft carriers into a battle that would destroy American sea power in the Pacific.*

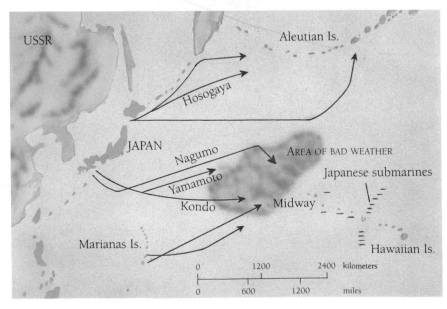

# MIDWAY

trap, the Japanese would destroy them with the warplanes from the aircraft carriers and the powerful guns of the battleships.

Yamamoto did not expect to meet the enemy in combat *before* reaching Midway. He did not know exactly where the American aircraft carriers were when he made his plans. But he and his advisers believed that the ships would be defending Pearl Harbor when he attacked Midway. Yamamoto based all his planning on this belief. However, to make doubly sure, he decided to send a smaller task force, commanded by Admiral Moshiro Hosogaya, into the northern Pacific. Their job was to attack the U.S. naval base at Dutch Harbor in the Aleutian Islands, 24 hours before the start of the attack on Midway. In this way Yamamoto hoped to draw the attention of the American commanders away from Midway. He thought that U.S. Admiral Nimitz would send ships and aircraft to Dutch Harbor, since an invasion of the Aleutian Islands would threaten Alaska and Canada.

▼ *An American warplane flies over the Aleutian Islands during the war.*

# Cracking the Japanese War Code

When Admiral Yamamoto and his staff drew up these plans, they made two big mistakes. In the first place, they thought they could keep their plan a secret and surprise the Americans as they had done six months earlier at Pearl Harbor. Second, they thought there would be no U.S. aircraft carriers close enough to Midway to fight back when they launched their attack. Yamamoto had been told that the *Yorktown* had been so badly damaged that it had sunk in the Coral Sea, which was not true. His staff told him that the other two carriers, the *Enterprise* and the *Hornet,* would be guarding Pearl Harbor itself.

However, American radio and **intelligence** experts had cracked the secret **code** that the Japanese used when sending messages to their ships. The Americans could now listen to enemy radio signals and work out the movements of Japanese ships.

## The American Trap

In May, the radio experts began to pick up messages that kept referring to a planned attack on a place called **AF**. Where and what was AF? Was it Australia? Was it Hawaii? Admiral Nimitz and his advisers thought not. They became convinced that AF must be the Japanese code name for Midway. But how could they make sure of this? They decided to set a trap. The U.S. engineers working on Midway were sent a secret cable telling them to broadcast a message to headquarters at Pearl Harbor.

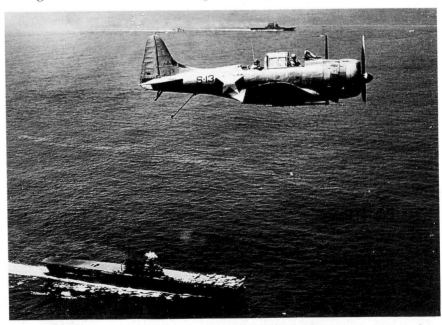

▶ *The Douglas Dauntless bombers were the most effective U.S. warplanes at the Battle of Midway.*

# MIDWAY

They were to say that Midway was having problems with its water supply. The Americans knew that the Japanese wireless operators would be listening to their radio signals. They would be sure to pass this message on to Admiral Yamamoto. To their great delight, a Japanese radio signal reported soon afterward that AF was having problems with its water supply! Nimitz and his senior commanders now knew for certain that AF was Midway. The Japanese attack was planned to take place in the first week of June.

## Repairing the *Yorktown*

By this time the badly damaged *Yorktown* had returned to Pearl Harbor. Despite protests that it could not be done, Nimitz ordered that the carrier be repaired and made ready for sea in three days. It was vital to get the carriers into position close to Midway well before the attack on June 4. The *Enterprise* and the *Hornet* left Pearl Harbor on May 28, a team of 1,400 workers, working long shifts, 24 hours a day, made the *Yorktown* ready for sea. The ship sailed two days later. On June 2, the three carriers met about 300 miles (500 kilometers) to the northeast of Midway. There they lay in wait for the Japanese invasion fleet.

▼ *The commanders of the U.S. carriers chose this position to the northeast of Midway because their planes could attack the Japanese carriers as soon as they came within range of the island. At the same time they were too far away from the approaching Japanese fleet to be spotted by Nagumo's scout planes until it was too late for him to change course.*

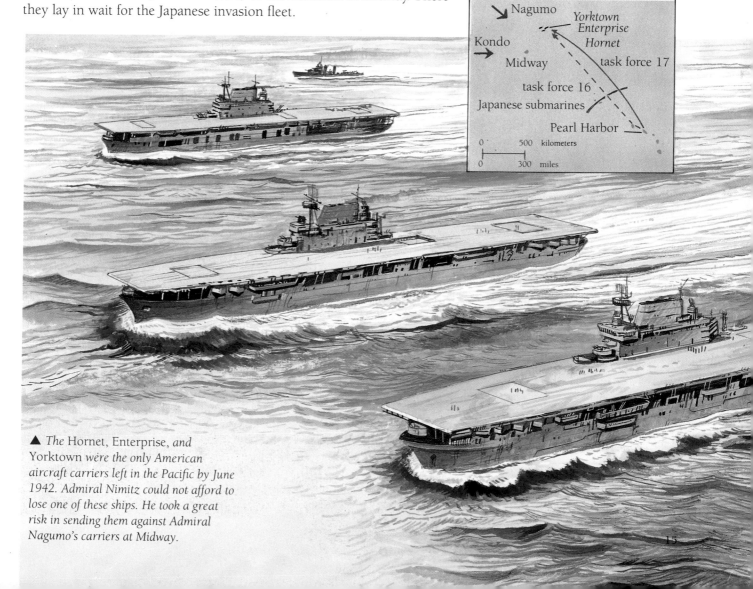

▲ *The* Hornet, Enterprise, *and* Yorktown *were the only American aircraft carriers left in the Pacific by June 1942. Admiral Nimitz could not afford to lose one of these ships. He took a great risk in sending them against Admiral Nagumo's carriers at Midway.*

15

▲ *Rear Admiral Spruance*

▲ *Vice Admiral Chuichi Nagumo*

# The Battle Fleets at Sea

Yamamoto took no risks. On June 2, submarines took up positions in a ring off the western coast of Hawaii. Their job was to report back immediately when they saw the American aircraft carriers leaving Pearl Harbor for Midway. They did not know that the U.S. carriers were already in position behind them, close to Midway.

Some of the Japanese admirals still wanted proof that the U.S. carriers were at Pearl Harbor. So Yamamoto arranged to send **flying boats** to the area. They would make **reconnaissance flights** over Hawaii to confirm that the U.S. carriers were still there. Since the flying boats could not reach Hawaii without refueling, Yamamoto sent a submarine laden with aviation fuel to meet them at the islands called French Frigate Shoals. This was halfway between Midway and Hawaii. When they got there, the Japanese found the islands already in American hands. The reconnaissance flights had to be canceled. Had they gone ahead, the Japanese would have known that the American aircraft carriers were at sea.

The absence of any firm information about the position of the American carriers worried Admiral Chuichi Nagumo. He was by nature a very cautious man. He told his staff to organize a series of air patrols to search the seas for the Americans as they approached Midway.

Admiral Nimitz, too, had organized reconnaissance flights to tell him when, and from which direction, the Japanese warships were approaching. At 9:00 A.M. on June 3, **Ensign** Jack Reid sighted Admiral Kondo's invasion force about 682 miles (1,100 kilometers) west of Midway. Rear Admiral Frank Fletcher and Rear Admiral Raymond Spruance now knew that the Japanese aircraft carriers must be closer than this, since their attack on Midway would have to come first. The sighting helped the Americans get into position for the battle the next day.

The Americans divided their battle fleet into two groups. Rear Admiral Spruance commanded Task Force 16. It consisted of the aircraft carriers *Enterprise* and *Hornet,* together with destroyers and other warships to protect them against enemy submarines and battleships. The *Yorktown* headed Task Force 17 where it was the **flagship** of Rear Admiral Fletcher, the commander in chief of the operation. There were in total about 70 American warships, together with 233 aircraft on the three carriers.

More than 150 warships accompanied Admiral Nagumo's four aircraft carriers, the *Kaga, Akagi, Soryu,* and *Hiryu.* They carried about 300 fighters and bombers. The men who piloted these ships were much more experienced in naval warfare than the Americans. Many had taken part in the Pearl Harbor raid only six months earlier. They left Japan full of confidence. As the ships steamed across the Pacific, the men sang patriotic war songs, such as "I shall die only for the Emperor. I shall never look back." They were sure that victory would soon be theirs.

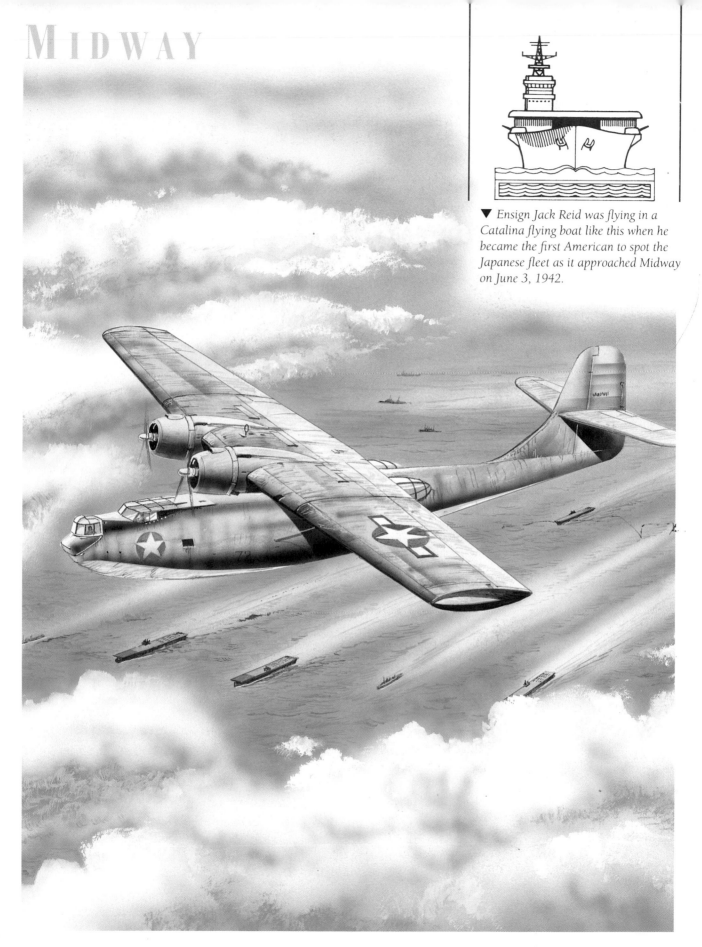

▼ Ensign Jack Reid was flying in a Catalina flying boat like this when he became the first American to spot the Japanese fleet as it approached Midway on June 3, 1942.

# First Strike at Midway

Meanwhile the *Akagi,* the flagship of Admiral Nagumo, commander of the Japanese carrier force, steamed on through pouring rain, fog, and rough seas. The sailors blessed the weather, since it hid the fact that a large invasion fleet was closing in on Midway. On June 3, 1942, Japanese warships and planes attacked the Aleutians according to plan. Although this caused some alarm in the United States, Admiral Nimitz ignored it. He knew the main Japanese attack was aimed at Midway.

▶ *The Japanese Zero fighters, seen here preparing to take off from an aircraft carrier during the Battle of Midway, were fast (about 344 mph [550 kph]), and very maneuverable. They were armed with two machine guns and two cannons. These fighters outclassed all Allied fighter aircraft until 1943.*

## The Battle Begins

At daybreak on June 4, 1942, the sea was calm and the skies were clear. It was only 4:30 A.M., but on board all four Japanese carriers the scene was one of hectic activity and excitement. Warplanes, laden with bombs and fuel, were taking off at rapid intervals for Midway. Instead of launching all his aircraft at once, however, the cautious Nagumo kept 93 of them back. These warplanes were loaded with torpedoes and special bombs that could pierce the thick armor plating of a ship. Nagumo wanted them to be ready in case the American aircraft carriers were seen.

Two hours later, at about 6:30 A.M., the strike force of 108 warplanes, led by Lieutenant Joichi Tomonaga, reached Midway. They badly damaged the U.S. military base there, destroying aircraft hangars, a hospital, and a number of storage tanks and depots. But antiaircraft fire and attacks by some of the American fighters based at Midway shot down about one third of the Japanese strike force. Tomonaga could see that the runway was still in use. He sent a radio signal to Nagumo to say that a second air strike was needed to destroy the runway.

# MIDWAY

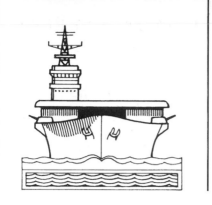

◀ *Smoke rises from the burning fuel dumps and aircraft hangars on Midway after the Japanese attack on June 4, 1942.*

## A Second Strike?

Nagumo now had a difficult problem. The 93 warplanes still on board his ships had been fitted with torpedoes and **armor-piercing** bombs. These were intended for attacking ships, and were useless against targets on land. To attack Midway, the planes would have to be taken below deck, unloaded, and then rearmed with bombs that could shatter buildings and destroy the runway. This would cause a delay and would also leave him without planes to attack the American carriers if they were found while the second raid was taking place.

At 7:10 A.M., however, as Nagumo was wondering what to do, there was an air raid. Some American bombers had taken off from Midway as soon as the **radar** there had identified Tomonaga's strike force. Although the American bombers did no damage, the fact that they could take off from Midway made up Nagumo's mind. A second strike was definitely needed. None of the scout planes searching the seas had seen any enemy warships, so at 7:15 A.M. Nagumo ordered the bombers to be taken below deck and loaded with bombs for Midway. This would also clear the flight decks to allow Tomonaga's returning planes to land.

◀ *A Grumman F4F Wildcat fighter returns to the airstrip at Midway after attacking the incoming Japanese warplanes. Midway was like a fourth American aircraft carrier during the battle but with a difference. It was unsinkable!*

# Admiral Nagumo's Dilemma

At 7:28 A.M., while the second-strike warplanes were being rearmed, Nagumo received alarming news. Ten U.S. warships had been sighted by the pilot of a scout plane. The news struck Nagumo "like a bolt from the blue." He told the pilot to check whether there were any carriers among the ten warships. While he waited, he made up his mind. At 7:45 A.M. he ordered a halt to the rearming of the warplanes. At 8:20 A.M. the pilot reported back, "The enemy ships are accompanied by what appears to be an aircraft carrier."

In fact, there were two carriers. The pilot had seen the ships of Rear Admiral Spruance's Task Force 16. Had he looked more closely, he could have given Nagumo much more worrying news. The flight decks of the American carriers were clear of aircraft. Their bombers were already looking for Nagumo and his carriers.

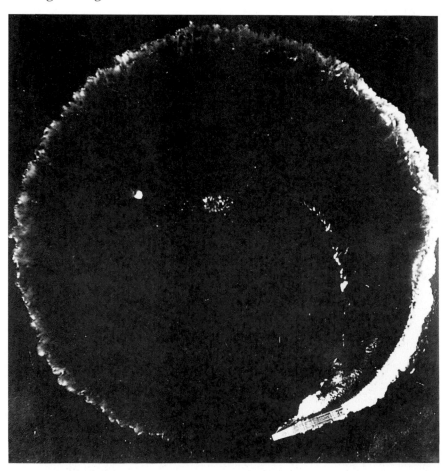

▶ *Taking off into the wind gives a plane extra lift. This is especially important on an aircraft carrier, with its short runway. This photograph shows the white trail made by the propellers of the Japanese aircraft carrier* Soryu. *The ship was* **turning into the wind** *to launch its warplanes.*

# MIDWAY

## The American Plan

An American plane had first spotted the Japanese carrier fleet at 5:34 A.M. When Tomonaga's strike force began bombing Midway an hour later, Spruance worked out roughly when they would be returning to their carriers. Having flown to Midway and back, they would be short of fuel. Clearing the flight decks to let returning crews land had one big drawback. It made aircraft carriers sitting ducks if an enemy attacked.

This is why Spruance turned his ships into the wind just after 7:00 A.M. He ordered the 116 warplanes on board to take off. Their instructions were simple. They were to destroy the Japanese aircraft carriers.

## Nagumo's Decision

At 8:20 A.M., Nagumo was unaware of the approach of the American warplanes. However, he knew now that an American aircraft carrier was within range of his own ships and that its commander would have heard by radio that Japanese warplanes had attacked Midway. He had every reason, therefore, to expect an enemy attack at any time. What should he do? Should he order the second-strike warplanes to be unloaded yet again and reloaded with torpedoes to attack the American aircraft carrier? Admiral Yamaguchi on the *Hiryu* suggested that since some of the warplanes on his own ship were still loaded with torpedoes, they could be sent immediately to mount an attack.

Nagumo did not wish to launch an attack with only a handful of planes. Instead, he decided to let Tomonaga's planes land first. While they were landing, the bombers below could be armed with torpedoes. Then while they attacked the American aircraft carrier, the first-strike warplanes could be refueled and loaded with bombs. These planes would complete the destruction of Midway later in the morning.

▲ *An aircraft carrier is an air force base as well as a ship. It carries a crew of 3,000 or more people, doing many different jobs, such as working as a pilot, aircraft engineer, ship's engineer, gunner, cook, or clerk.*

▲ *Zero fighter in action at the Battle of Midway*

# The American Attack

The next sixty minutes or so were chaotic on board the Japanese aircraft carriers. The Zero fighters took off to patrol the skies in case of an American attack. Then Tomonaga's first-strike planes began to land, while below deck huge piles of bombs were hastily stacked to one side as the second-strike warplanes were rearmed with torpedoes.

The American planes, meanwhile, had had problems finding the Japanese ships, since they had changed speed and direction (see map on page 25). Half the U.S. planes went the wrong way and had to land on Midway. The others spotted Nagumo and launched their attacks. The first wave to do so was a squadron of Devastator torpedo bombers. They were no match for the much faster, more agile, and better-armed Japanese Zero fighters that protected the skies above the Japanese carrier fleet. None of the American planes got near enough to attack the carriers. All were shot down. All the crews died except one man.

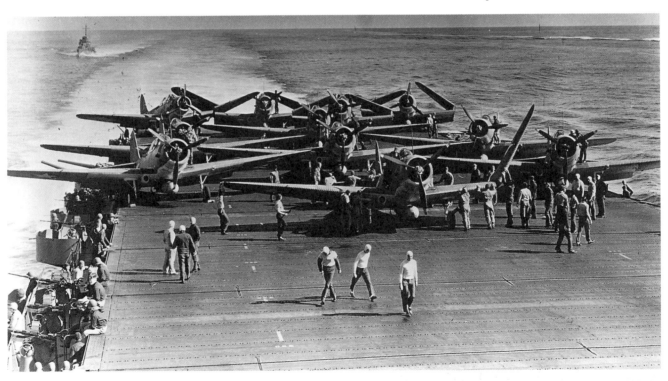

▲ *These American Devastator torpedo bombers were preparing to take off from the* Enterprise. *More than 30 pilots did not return from the attack on the Japanese carrier fleet.*

A second and a third American attack fared just as badly. Nagumo and his staff and crews now thought that the worst was over. The Japanese ships were turning into the wind to launch the second-strike torpedo bombers, and Tomonaga's planes had landed and were being refueled. It was 10:20 A.M. Nagumo did not know, however, that 37 American Dauntless dive-bombers (page 4) were even now approaching his carrier fleet from a height of 19,000 feet (6,000 meters).

# MIDWAY

◀ *This is a pilot's view of the Battle of Midway. It was taken from a Dauntless dive-bomber and shows a burning Japanese aircraft carrier far below.*

## The "Hell-Divers"

"Hell-Divers!" screamed a Japanese lookout. Mitsuo Fuchida said he "looked up to see three black enemy planes plummeting toward our ship." In the space of five minutes or so, eight bombs fell on the *Kaga* and three each on the *Soryu* and *Akagi*. It was "just like hell," recalled a Japanese officer. The captain of the *Soryu* went down with his ship and Admiral Nagumo would have done so, too, but officers fighting through flames dragged him away from the *Akagi*.

All three Japanese carriers were damaged beyond repair. They sank within 24 hours. In only five minutes the Japanese war effort had been severely beaten.

◀ *This photograph shows a Japanese cruiser, heavily damaged by American action at Midway.*

23

# Hiryu and Yorktown Are Sunk

One of the four Japanese carriers, the *Hiryu*, was some distance in front of the others. This ship escaped the American onslaught, and its commander, Admiral Yamaguchi, launched a counterattack. He sent his warplanes off at about 11:00 A.M., only half an hour after the American attack on the *Kaga, Soryu,* and *Akagi*.

Instead of finding the *Enterprise* and the *Hornet,* however, the Japanese planes discovered the ill-fated *Yorktown*. American Wildcat fighters shot down eight of the Japanese intruders, but another eight got through. They scored three direct hits at about midday and damaged the *Yorktown* so severely that the carrier came to a halt. About two hours later, the *Hiryu* launched a second attack. Ten torpedo bombers, protected by six Zeros, came in very low and fired torpedoes from just above sea level. They scored a direct hit, gashing the side of the ship. Water streamed into the gaping hole and caused the ship to **list** (tilt over). It was so badly damaged that the crew had to abandon ship. Like the three Japanese carriers, the *Yorktown* soon sank.

▲ *Low-flying Japanese torpedo bombers from the* Hiryu *attack the* Yorktown. *The black puffs of smoke show the amount of heavy antiaircraft fire they had to avoid in order to fire their missiles.*

Meanwhile, Dauntless dive-bombers from the *Enterprise* and *Yorktown* had located the *Hiryu*. They launched another successful attack at 5:00 P.M. that resulted in the sinking of this, the last of the four Japanese aircraft carriers. Admiral Yamaguchi, true to the traditions of the **samurai,** the ancient Japanese warriors, went down with his ship rather than admit defeat.

# MIDWAY

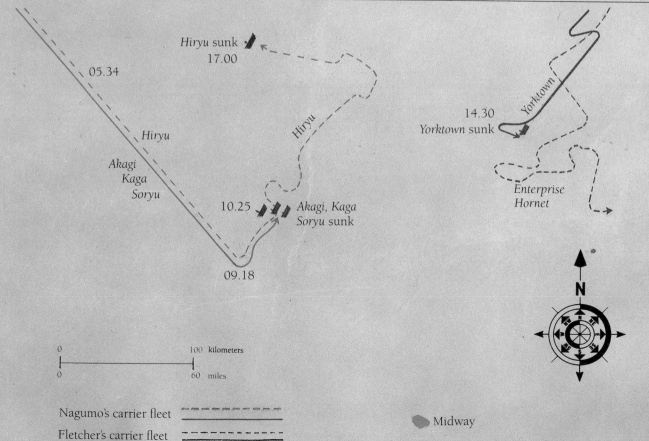

◄ *The deck of the Yorktown tilts over as the crew wait to abandon their ship. Yorktown was the only American aircraft carrier to be sunk at Midway. The Japanese lost four carriers.*

## An American Victory

Unlike the Battle of the Coral Sea a month earlier, there was a clear winner at the Battle of Midway. The Japanese had lost four first-class aircraft carriers, 332 aircraft, and more than 3,500 highly trained men. American casualties were also high — one aircraft carrier, the *Yorktown*, 147 aircraft, and 307 men. But although these losses were severe, they were nowhere near as catastrophic as those suffered by the Japanese.

▼ *You can see from this map of the Battle of Midway why it took the American warplanes a long time to locate Nagumo's carriers.*

Hiryu sunk
17.00

05.34

*Hiryu*

*Hiryu*

*Akagi*
*Kaga*
*Soryu*

10.25

*Akagi, Kaga Soryu sunk*

09.18

14.30
Yorktown sunk

*Yorktown*

*Enterprise*
*Hornet*

N

| 0 | | 100 kilometers |
| 0 | | 60 miles |

Nagumo's carrier fleet

Fletcher's carrier fleet

Midway

# Turning Point

Admiral Yamamoto found it difficult to realize that he was defeated. His battleships and cruisers still heavily outnumbered the ships in the American fleet and had much greater firing power. This is why he tried to draw the U.S. task forces into battle. But Spruance withdrew the American ships, knowing that to confront Yamamoto and his battleships would be too much for his forces.

Yamamoto also knew that he would have to call off the invasion. If he waited for the Americans to regroup, then their carriers *Enterprise* and *Hornet* would launch an attack on his battleships. And he was now without Nagumo's Zero fighters to protect the ships.

So, despite their colossal firepower, the mighty Japanese battleships had to retreat or face the American aircraft carriers. The Battle of Midway had proved beyond a doubt that the battleship was now an out-of-date war weapon. Together with the Battle of the Coral Sea, this battle had changed the face of naval warfare.

Yamamoto had set out to destroy the U.S. Navy. Instead, the Japanese fleet had been massively defeated in a contest of skill, strength, and luck. Since that time, historians have called Midway the most decisive battle of World War II. The tide of war in the Pacific had turned.

▼ *The* Yorktown *on fire after the Japanese attack. Even ships of this size and quality could be sunk by a single torpedo.*

# MIDWAY

◀ The Enterprise was the only carrier at Midway to survive World War II.

From now on the Americans were mostly on the attack, and the Japanese had to defend themselves. Yet only a few weeks earlier, even Australia had felt threatened by the Japanese.

The war was not over, of course. The Japanese still had more aircraft carriers than the Americans. They had a powerful navy and a very efficient army. For the time being, however, the U.S. Navy could face the Japanese on equal terms, since Japan had lost four of its best aircraft carriers and a large number of its most experienced pilots. Ships of this size and pilots of that quality could not be replaced for months, even years. The Japanese were not able to keep up with American industry in building new ships and aircraft.

◀ This Japanese war poster praising the country's airmen was painted in 1942. The cost and time involved in training men to become skilled naval pilots was such that the Japanese could ill afford to lose so many in just one battle.

27

# Victory at a Cost

The Americans followed up their victory at Midway. In August 1942 they landed on the island of Guadalcanal. This was the first of a number of Pacific islands that were taken by American marines in the face of strong Japanese opposition. In the next three years the Americans captured many other Pacific islands. They called it **"island hopping."** Each new island was used as a base from which to capture the next island. American aircraft carriers played a vital part in this type of warfare, since their air power helped the U.S. marines to win the war on land.

In 1944, American forces recaptured the Philippines, and in 1945 went on to take two islands on the fringe of Japan itself, Okinawa and Iwo Jima. After the defeat of Nazi Germany in May 1945, the Americans were able to concentrate all their efforts on the war in the Far East. The U.S. commanders began to make plans for an invasion of Japan in 1946. However, they knew by now that this would be extremely costly in both men and materials. The Japanese soldiers who had defended the islands of Iwo Jima and Okinawa had fought with great ferocity. Most had refused to surrender. More than 100,000 Japanese soldiers and about 12,000 American soldiers had died on Okinawa. Allied commanders feared they might lose as many as one million men if Japan itself was invaded. They knew that the Japanese would fight to the last man, woman, and child rather than surrender.

▼ *American marines invading the Solomon Islands in 1942*

# MIDWAY

## The Secret Weapon

The new U.S. president, Harry S Truman, had inherited a secret weapon of war—the first nuclear weapons. In August 1945, Truman ordered the dropping of the atom bomb on the Japanese city of **Hiroshima.** It was followed a few days later by a second atom bomb on the city of **Nagasaki.** The destruction caused and the loss of life was the worst in history. The emperor of Japan felt the country had no alternative. Japan surrendered on August 14, 1945. World War II was over.

## What Happened to the Admirals?

Unlike Admiral Nimitz and Rear Admiral Spruance, neither of the two Japanese commanders most closely associated with the Battle of Midway lived to see Japan's surrender at the end of the war. In April 1943, Admiral Isoroku Yamamoto went on a tour of Japanese bases in the Solomon Islands. The Allied code breakers were able to work out from careless Japanese radio signals the route he was taking. He was killed when the bomber plane he was traveling in was shot down by American fighter planes. After his defeat at Midway, Admiral Chuichi Nagumo was given a less important command. In July 1944 he shot himself rather than be captured by American soldiers. Both Admiral Nimitz and Rear Admiral Spruance were promoted. Nimitz became a five-star admiral in 1944, when Spruance took his place as commander in chief of the Pacific fleet.

▲ *U.S. soldiers raise the American flag on the summit of Mount Suribachi during the battle for the island of Iwo Jima in February 1945. Island hopping like this was only possible thanks to the air support provided by the American aircraft carriers.*

◄ *The official surrender of the Japanese took place on board the battleship* Missouri *on September 2, 1945. Fleet Admiral Nimitz was there. His victory at Midway helped to bring the war to an end.*

# Glossary

**admiral:** a top ranking officer in a navy

**AF:** the Japanese code name for Midway

**aircraft carrier:** a ship that can launch and recover aircraft on its flight deck

**Aleutian Islands:** a group of islands in the North Pacific linking North America with Asia

**armor-piercing bomb:** a bomb designed to pierce through the thick armor plating used to protect a ship against enemy attack

**battleship:** a very large warship armed with powerful guns

**B-25:** a twin-engined bomber in service with the U.S. Air Force in 1942

**code:** a way of sending secret messages so that an enemy or rival cannot read or understand them

**Commonwealth:** the countries, such as Australia, India, and Canada, that used to form the British Empire

**destroyer:** a small, fast warship designed to destroy enemy submarines (and other ships) using its speed to make an attack and then get away

**dive-bomber:** a bomber that flies at a great height. When it attacks, it dives downward at a very steep angle, thus increasing its speed.

**ensign:** a junior officer in the U.S. Navy

**fighter:** an aircraft used primarily for attacking other aircraft, such as a bomber or a transport plane

**firepower:** in naval warfare, the capacity of a ship or gun to fire missiles, such as shells, bullets, or torpedos. The more effective the explosive power and distance traveled by the missiles, the greater the firepower.

**flagship:** the ship used by an admiral for his headquarters

**flattop:** popular nickname for an aircraft carrier

**fleet:** a large group of warships fighting under the same command

**flight deck:** the flat deck from which aircraft are launched on an aircraft carrier

**flying boat:** an airplane that takes off and lands on water instead of on land

**hangar:** a large shed where aircraft are housed

**Hawaiian Islands:** the group of islands to the east of Midway that now make up the state of Hawaii

**Hiroshima:** a city in Japan that was largely destroyed in August 1945 by the first atomic bomb dropped in warfare

**intelligence:** in wartime this means a department whose job it is to try to find out what the enemy is up to

**island hopping:** used to describe the way in which the American marines used one adjacent island after another to drive the Japanese back toward Japan

**Japanese High Command:** the high-ranking officers who worked under the emperor to direct the war effort in Japan

**list:** in a ship this means tilting over to one side

**Midway:** two tiny islands with an area of 2.2 square miles (5.5 square kilometers) in the middle of the Pacific

**minesweeper:** a ship that has been specially designed so that it can discover and deal with mines (floating bombs) that have been laid by an enemy

**Nagasaki:** a city in Japan that was largely destroyed in August 1945 by the second atomic bomb dropped in warfare

# MIDWAY

**Pearl Harbor:** large deep-water harbor on the island of Oahu in Hawaii. Used by the United States as a naval base.

**radar:** an electronic device that warns of the approach of moving objects, such as an aircraft or a ship

**radio signal:** message sent by radio, often in code

**reconnaissance flight:** an airplane equipped with a camera that is used to take aerial photographs of the land or sea occupied by enemy forces

**samurai:** medieval warriors of Japan whose code of warlike conduct was often imitated by the Japanese armed services during World War II

**task force:** a group of soldiers, sailors, or airmen formed to accomplish a particular task, such as the seizure of an island like Midway

**torpedo bomber:** an aircraft designed to fly at low levels so that it can fire a torpedo—a very long, pointed bomb—at a low angle so that it can penetrate the hull of a ship

**turning into the wind:** moving an aircraft carrier around so that aircraft taking off can fly head-on into the wind to give them the extra lift they need

## Further reading

Denavey, John. *Nineteen Forty-One: America Goes to War.* New York: Walker and Co., 1991.

Dunnahoo, Terry. *Pearl Harbor: America Enters the War.* New York: Franklin Watts, 1991.

Farris, John. *Hiroshima.* San Diego: Lucent Books, 1990.

Ferry, Charles. *Raspberry One.* New York: Houghton Mifflin Co., 1983.

Harris, Sarah. *How and Why: The Second World War.* North Pomfret, Vermont: Trafalgar Square, 1989.

Hills, C. A. *The Second World War.* North Pomfret, Vermont: Trafalgar Square, 1985.

Hoare, Stephen. *Hiroshima.* North Pomfret, Vermont: Trafalgar Square, 1987.

McGowan, Tom. *Midway and Guadalcanal.* New York: Franklin Watts, 1984.

Messenger, Charles. *The Second World War.* New York: Franklin Watts, 1987.

Shapiro, William E. *Pearl Harbor.* New York: Franklin Watts, 1984.

Tames, Richard. *Japan Since 1945.* North Pomfret, Vermont: Trafalgar Square, 1989.

Tsuchiya, Yukio. *Faithful Elephants.* New York: Houghton Mifflin Co., 1988.

## Films

You may also be able to see on television or on video the movie *Battle of Midway*, which starred Charlton Heston and Henry Fonda. Look out, too, for the film about Pearl Harbor called *Tora! Tora! Tora!*, which featured many leading Japanese as well as American actors.

# Index